READING POWER

Earth Rocks!

Gems

Holly Cefrey

The Rosen Publishing Group's
PowerKids Press™
New York

Published in 2003 by The Rosen Publishing Group, Inc.
29 East 21st Street, New York, NY 10010

First Edition

Book Design: Mindy Liu

Photo Credits: Cover © Image Bank; pp. 4–5 © James L. Stanfield/ National Geographic Image Collection; pp. 6–7 © Lester V. Bergman/ Corbis; p. 7 (top) Adriana Skura; pp. 8–9 © Gallo Images/Corbis; pp. 10–11 © E.R. Degginger/Animals Animals; p. 13 (top) © Layne Kennedy/Corbis: p 13 (bottom) © Robert Holmes/Corbis; p. 14 © Raymond Gehman/Corbis; p. 15 © Helen Thompson/Animals Animals; p. 16 © Charles O'Rear/Corbis; p. 17 © Adam Woolfitt/Corbis; pp. 18, 19 © Erich Lessing/Art Resource, NY; p. 20 © Jonathan Blair/Corbis; p. 21 © Bettmann/Corbis

Library of Congress Cataloging-in-Publication Data

Cefrey, Holly.
Gems / Holly Cefrey.
    p. cm. – (Earth rocks!)
Includes bibliographical references and index.
ISBN 0-8239-6467-1 (library binding)
1. Precious stones–Juvenile literature. 2. Mineralogy–Juvenile literature. [1. Precious stones. 2. Mineralogy.] I. Title.
QE392.2 .C44 2003
553.8–dc21
                                    2002000101

Contents

Gems

There are many kinds of gems. Most gems are made in rocks. However, some gems can be made by plants and animals, too.

Gems are valued for their beauty.

A mineral is solid matter that comes from the earth. There are more than 2,000 different minerals. But only 100 of these minerals are called gems. Most people think that gems are worth more money than other minerals. Most people also think that gems are very beautiful.

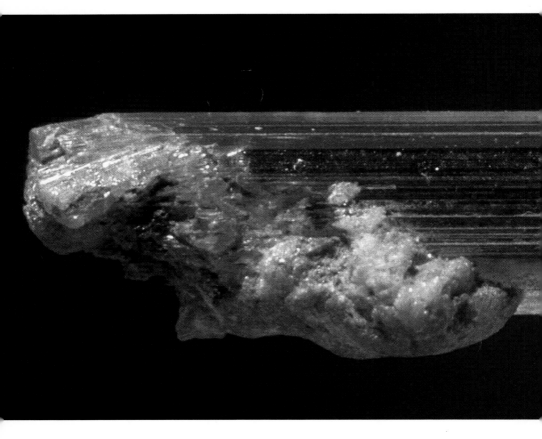

Emeralds come from the mineral beryl (BEHR-uhl).

How Gems Are Made

Most gems are made from minerals that are found in many different kinds of rocks. Heat and pressure deep inside Earth can change the minerals in rocks into very hard, beautiful crystals. These crystals are gems.

This diamond is still in the rock where it formed.

Sometimes, when rocks are formed, they have holes inside made by gas bubbles. Water that is rich in minerals can get inside the holes in the rocks.

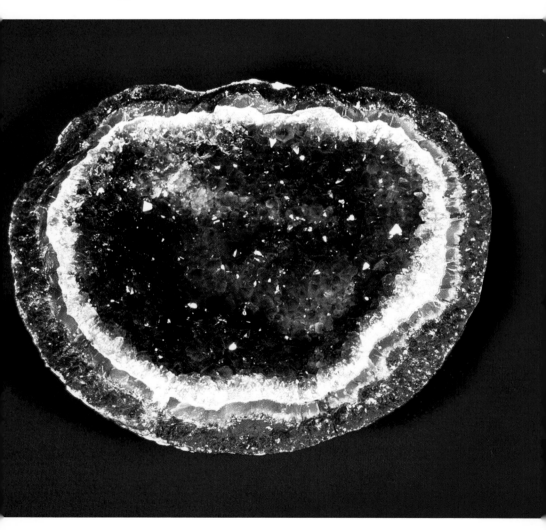

Gems can be formed inside the holes from the minerals in the water.

Sometimes, gems may be formed from mineral-rich water in some rocks.

Gems are also made by animals and plants. Pearls *(PUHRLZ)* are made inside clams, oysters, and mussels. Coral *(KOR-uhl)* is made from the skeletons of tiny sea animals. Amber *(AM-buhr)* is what is left of the sap of very old pine trees. Jet is a black-colored gem made from very old wood, much like coal.

The Fact Box

Pearls were once the most costly gems on Earth. A Roman general once paid for an entire war by selling one pearl earring.

Sometimes, insects get trapped in tree sap. Over time, the sap turns into amber with the insect inside.

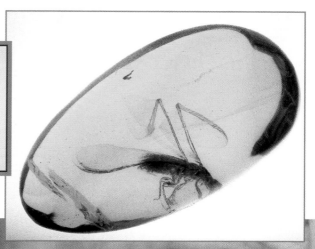

Pearls are made when a piece of sand or other matter gets inside an animal's shell. The animal is bothered by the sand and covers the piece of sand with special matter that it makes. In about seven years, the matter builds up to make a pearl.

Finding Gems

Many gems are hard to find because they are buried deep inside Earth. Some gems are found in rivers. Running water may force gems from layers of rock and leave them on the bottom of a river. People search through mud and sand taken from river bottoms to find gems.

Some gems can be found by looking through sand, rock, and earth taken from river bottoms.

Diamonds are found about 90 miles below ground. Miners may dig up 500 tons of rock to get only one ounce of diamond. In one year, about 21 tons of diamond are found around the world.

Polishing and Cutting

Most gems that people find look dull. These gems are polished to make them shiny and smooth. The gems are also cut to shape them and make them sparkle.

These diamonds have not been cut and polished.

The Fact Box

Gems are weighed in carats. *Carat* comes from the word for carob bean in the Greek language. One carat is about the weight of one carob bean.

Gems may be cut to have either flat or round sides.

Using Gems

People have been using gems to make jewelry and art for about 20,000 years. Many people have also believed that gems have special powers. They thought that some gems, such as jade and garnet, could heal illness.

This crown from eastern Europe is more than 650 years old. Many different gems were used to make it.

The ancient Egyptians used lapis lazuli in their artwork.

The Fact Box

The ancient Egyptians crushed a blue gem, lapis lazuli *(LAHP-uhs LA-zuh-lee)*, into a powder and used it as eye shadow. In the 1400s, artists in Europe used the same crushed gem to make blue paint.

Today, people also use gems for tools. Diamonds are used in tools that can cut through other objects. Rubies are used in lasers. Gems are both beautiful and useful.

Sometimes, diamonds are used to make telephone wires. Diamond is the hardest natural matter on Earth.

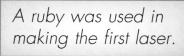
A ruby was used in making the first laser.

Glossary

carat (**kar**-at) the measurement used to weigh gems

carob bean (**kar**-uhb **been**) the seed of a carob tree that is used to make a food much like chocolate

crystals (**krihs**-tlz) hard, usually clear, matter that have angles and flat surfaces

gem (**jehm**) a hard, colorful mineral or other matter; most gems are worth a lot of money

laser (**lay**-zuhr) a tool with a thin, powerful beam of light that is used to cut things

minerals (**mihn**-uhr-uhlz) solid matter that comes from the earth

polished (**pahl**-ihshd) to have been made smooth and shiny

pressure (**prehsh**-uhr) the continued action of a weight or force

sparkle (**spahr**-kuhl) to give off bright light

Resources

Books

Eyewitness: Crystal & Gem
by R. F. Symes
Dorling Kindersley Publishing (2000)

Gemstones
by Emma Foa
Dorling Kindersley Publishing (1997)

Web Sites

Due to the changing nature of Internet links, PowerKids
Press has developed an on-line list of Web sites related
to the subjects of this book. This site is updated regularly.
Please use this link to access the list:

http://www.powerkidslinks.com/ear/gem/

Index

A
animal, 4, 12–13

C
crystals, 8

D
diamond, 9, 15–16, 20

J
jewelry, 18

L
laser, 20–21

M
mineral, 6–8, 10–11
money, 6

P
pearl, 12–13
plants, 4, 12
pressure, 8

T
tools, 20

Word Count: 431

Note to Librarians, Teachers, and Parents

If reading is a challenge, Reading Power is a solution! Reading Power is perfect for readers who want high-interest subject matter at an accessible reading level. These fact-filled, photo-illustrated books are designed for readers who want straightforward vocabulary, engaging topics, and a manageable reading experience. With clear picture/text correspondence, leveled Reading Power books put the reader in charge. Now readers have the power to get the information they want and the skills they need in a user-friendly format.